Francis Frith's
CUMBRIA

PHOTOGRAPHIC MEMORIES

Francis Frith's CUMBRIA

Roly Smith

First published in the United Kingdom in 2000 by
Frith Book Company Ltd

Hardback Edition 2000
ISBN 1-85937-101-9

Paperback Edition 2002
ISBN 1-85937-621-5

Text and Design copyright © Frith Book Company Ltd
Photographs copyright © The Francis Frith Collection

The Frith photographs and the Frith logo are reproduced under licence from
Heritage Photographic Resources Ltd, the owners of the Frith archive and trademarks

All rights reserved. No photograph in this publication may be sold to a third party other than in
the original form of this publication, or framed for sale to a third party.
No parts of this publication may be reproduced, stored in a retrieval system, or
transmitted, in any form, or by any means, electronic, mechanical, photocopying, recording or
otherwise, without the prior permission of the publishers and copyright holder.

British Library Cataloguing in Publication Data

Francis Frith's Cumbria
Roly Smith

Frith Book Company Ltd
Frith's Barn, Teffont,
Salisbury, Wiltshire SP3 5QP
Tel: +44 (0) 1722 716 376
Email: info@francisfrith.co.uk
www.francisfrith.co.uk

Printed and bound in Great Britain

AS WITH ANY HISTORICAL DATABASE THE FRITH ARCHIVE IS CONSTANTLY BEING CORRECTED AND IMPROVED
AND THE PUBLISHERS WOULD WELCOME INFORMATION ON OMISSIONS OR INACCURACIES

Contents

Francis Frith: Victorian Pioneer   7

Frith's Archive - A Unique Legacy   10

Cumbria - An Introduction   12

The Lakes   16

North Cumbria   48

The Cumbrian Pennines   66

South Cumbria   79

West Cumbria   110

Index   115

Free Mounted Print Voucher   119

FRANCIS FRITH: *Victorian Pioneer*

FRANCIS FRITH, Victorian founder of the world-famous photographic archive, was a complex and multitudinous man. A devout Quaker and a highly successful Victorian businessman, he was both philosophic by nature and pioneering in outlook.

By 1855 Francis Frith had already established a wholesale grocery business in Liverpool, and sold it for the astonishing sum of £200,000, which is the equivalent today of over £15,000,000. Now a multi-millionaire, he was able to indulge his passion for travel. As a child he had pored over travel books written by early explorers, and his fancy and imagination had been stirred by family holidays to the sublime mountain regions of Wales and Scotland. 'What a land of spirit-stirring and enriching scenes and places!' he had written. He was to return to these scenes of grandeur in later years to 'recapture the thousands of vivid and tender memories', but with a different purpose. Now in his thirties, and captivated by the new science of photography, Frith set out on a series of pioneering journeys to the Nile regions that occupied him from 1856 until 1860.

INTRIGUE AND ADVENTURE

He took with him on his travels a specially-designed wicker carriage that acted as both dark-room and sleeping chamber. These far-flung journeys were packed with intrigue and adventure. In his life story, written when he was sixty-three, Frith tells of being held captive by bandits, and of fighting 'an awful midnight battle to the very point of surrender with a deadly pack of hungry wild dogs'. Sporting flowing Arab costume, Frith arrived at Akaba by camel seventy years before Lawrence, where he encountered 'desert princes and rival sheikhs, blazing with jewel-hilted swords'.

During these extraordinary adventures he was assiduously exploring the desert regions bordering the Nile and patiently recording the antiquities and peoples with his camera. He was the first photographer to venture beyond the sixth cataract. Africa was still the mysterious 'Dark Continent', and Stanley and Livingstone's historic meeting was a decade into the future. The conditions for picture taking confound belief. He laboured for hours in his wicker dark-room in the sweltering heat of the desert, while the volatile chemicals fizzed dangerously in their trays. Often he was forced to work in remote tombs and caves where conditions were cooler. Back in London he exhibited his photographs and was 'rapturously cheered' by members of the Royal Society. His reputation as a photographer was made overnight. An eminent modern historian has likened their impact on the population of the time to that on our own generation of the first photographs taken on the surface of the moon.

VENTURE OF A LIFE-TIME

Characteristically, Frith quickly spotted the opportunity to create a new business as a specialist publisher of photographs. He lived in an era of immense and sometimes violent change. For the poor in the early part of Victoria's reign work was a drudge and the hours long, and people had precious little free time to enjoy themselves. Most had no transport other than a cart or gig at their disposal, and had not travelled far beyond the boundaries of their own town or village. However, by the 1870s, the railways had threaded their way across the country, and Bank Holidays and half-day Saturdays had been made obligatory by Act of Parliament. All of a sudden the ordinary working man and his family were able to enjoy days out and see a little more of the world.

With characteristic business acumen, Francis Frith foresaw that these new tourists would enjoy having souvenirs to commemorate their days out. In 1860 he married Mary Ann Rosling and set out with the intention of photographing every city, town and village in Britain. For the next thirty years he travelled the country by train and by pony and trap, producing fine photographs of seaside resorts and beauty spots that were keenly bought by millions of Victorians. These prints were painstakingly pasted into family albums and pored over during the dark nights of winter, rekindling precious memories of summer excursions.

THE RISE OF FRITH & CO

Frith's studio was soon supplying retail shops all over the country. To meet the demand he gathered about him a small team of photographers, and published the work of independent artist-photographers of the calibre of Roger Fenton and Francis Bedford. In order to gain some understanding of the scale of Frith's business one only has to look at the catalogue issued by Frith & Co in 1886: it runs to some 670

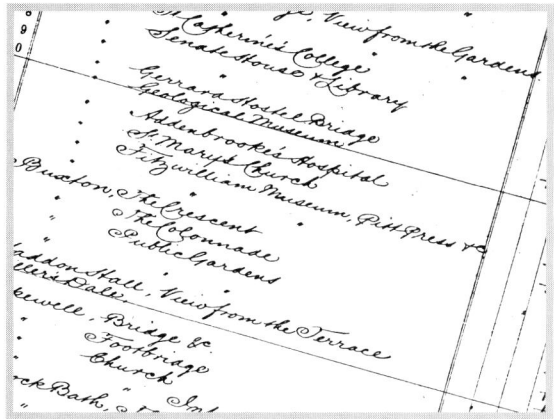

pages, listing not only many thousands of views of the British Isles but also many photographs of most European countries, and China, Japan, the USA and Canada – note the sample page shown above from the hand-written *Frith & Co* ledgers detailing pictures taken. By 1890 Frith had created the greatest specialist photographic publishing company in the world, with over 2,000 outlets – more than the combined number that Boots and WH Smith have today! The picture on the right shows the *Frith & Co* display board at Ingleton in the Yorkshire Dales. Beautifully constructed with mahogany frame and gilt inserts, it could display up to a dozen local scenes.

POSTCARD BONANZA

The ever-popular holiday postcard we know today took many years to develop. In 1870 the Post Office issued the first plain cards, with a pre-printed stamp on one face. In 1894 they allowed other publishers' cards to be sent through the mail with an attached adhesive halfpenny stamp. Demand grew rapidly, and in 1895 a new size of postcard was permitted called the court card, but there was little room for illustration. In 1899, a year after Frith's death, a new card measuring 5.5 x 3.5 inches became the standard format, but it was not until 1902 that the divided back came into being, with address and message on one face and a full-size illustration on the other. *Frith & Co* were in the vanguard of postcard development, and Frith's sons Eustace and Cyril continued their father's monumental task, expanding the number of views offered to the public and recording more and more places in Britain, as the coasts and countryside were opened up to mass travel.

Francis Frith died in 1898 at his villa in Cannes, his great project still growing. The archive he created continued in business for another seventy years. By 1970 it contained over a third of a million pictures of 7,000 cities, towns and villages. The massive photographic record Frith has left to us stands as a living monument to a special and very remarkable man.

Frith's Archive: *A Unique Legacy*

FRANCIS FRITH'S legacy to us today is of immense significance and value, for the magnificent archive of evocative photographs he created provides a unique record of change in 7,000 cities, towns and villages throughout Britain over a century and more. Frith and his fellow studio photographers revisited locations many times down the years to update their views, compiling for us an enthralling and colourful pageant of British life and character.

We tend to think of Frith's sepia views of Britain as nostalgic, for most of us use them to conjure up memories of places in our own lives with which we have family associations. It often makes us forget that to Francis Frith they were records of daily life as it was actually being lived in the cities, towns and villages of his day. The Victorian age was one of great and often bewildering change for ordinary people, and though the pictures evoke an impression of slower times, life was as busy and hectic as it is today.

We are fortunate that Frith was a photographer of the people, dedicated to recording the minutiae of everyday life. For it is this sheer wealth of visual data, the painstaking chronicle of changes in dress, transport, street layouts, buildings, housing, engineering and landscape that captivates us so much today. His remarkable images offer us a powerful link with the past and with the lives of our ancestors.

TODAY'S TECHNOLOGY

Computers have now made it possible for Frith's many thousands of images to be accessed almost instantly. In the Frith archive today, each photograph is carefully 'digitised' then stored on a CD Rom. Frith archivists can locate a single photograph amongst thousands within seconds. Views can be catalogued and sorted under a variety of categories of place and content to the immediate benefit of researchers. Inexpensive reference prints can be created for them at the touch of a mouse button, and a wide range of books and other printed materials assembled and published for a wider, more general readership - in the next twelve months over a hundred Frith local history titles will be published! The

See Frith at www.francisfrith.co.uk

day-to-day workings of the archive are very different from how they were in Francis Frith's time: imagine the herculean task of sorting through eleven tons of glass negatives as Frith had to do to locate a particular sequence of pictures! Yet the archive still prides itself on maintaining the same high standards of excellence laid down by Francis Frith, including the painstaking cataloguing and indexing of every view.

It is curious to reflect on how the internet now allows researchers in America and elsewhere greater instant access to the archive than Frith himself ever enjoyed. Many thousands of individual views can be called up on screen within seconds on one of the Frith internet sites, enabling people living continents away to revisit the streets of their ancestral home town, or view places in Britain where they have enjoyed holidays. Many overseas researchers welcome the chance to view special theme selections, such as transport, sports, costume and ancient monuments.

We are certain that Francis Frith would have heartily approved of these modern developments, for he himself was always working at the very limits of Victorian photographic technology.

THE VALUE OF THE ARCHIVE TODAY

Because of the benefits brought by the computer, Frith's images are increasingly studied by social historians, by researchers into genealogy and ancestory, by architects, town planners, and by teachers and schoolchildren involved in local history projects. In addition, the archive offers every one of us a unique opportunity to examine the places where we and our families have lived and worked down the years. Immensely successful in Frith's own era, the archive is now, a century and more on, entering a new phase of popularity.

THE PAST IN TUNE WITH THE FUTURE

Historians consider the Francis Frith Collection to be of prime national importance. It is the only archive of its kind remaining in private ownership and has been valued at a million pounds. However, this figure is now rapidly increasing as digital technology enables more and more people around the world to enjoy its benefits.

Francis Frith's archive is now housed in an historic timber barn in the beautiful village of Teffont in Wiltshire. Its founder would not recognize the archive office as it is today. In place of the many thousands of dusty boxes containing glass plate negatives and an all-pervading odour of photographic chemicals, there are now ranks of computer screens. He would be amazed to watch his images travelling round the world at unimaginable speeds through network and internet lines.

The archive's future is both bright and exciting. Francis Frith, with his unshakeable belief in making photographs available to the greatest number of people, would undoubtedly approve of what is being done today with his lifetime's work. His photographs, depicting our shared past, are now bringing pleasure and enlightenment to millions around the world a century and more after his death.

Cumbria – *An Introduction*

FOR MOST PEOPLE, Cumbria means the Lake District - that gnarled knot of fells and lakes west of the M6 motorway which constitutes the highest land in England. This is the Cumbria which the tourist board, with some justification, calls 'the most beautiful corner of England': the Cumbria of Wordsworth and the Lakeland poets, and the Cumbria of the modern tourist picture postcards.

But as true lovers of Cumbria know, there is much, much more to the county than that, as this book of photographs, mainly from the turn of the 19th century, will attempt to show. It ranges from the towns of the industrial west coast, where coal and iron ore was transported from once-busy ports like Maryport and Whitehaven, to the very borders with Scotland, influenced and governed for so many centuries by the red sandstone walls of Carlisle and its castle, and by the western sector of Hadrian's Wall before that.

To the south, there are the copper-bearing hills around Coniston, for so long part of the County Palatine of Lancaster, and the historic area of the Furness peninsula, still known sometimes as 'Lancashire-over-the-Sands'. Then, in sharp contrast, there is the Cumbria of the northern Pennines east of the M6, taking in the smooth, rolling fells of the Howgills and the bleak, high moors around Alston. Here lead extraction was the major industry for centuries, and the snow lies late in the lee of hills like Cross Fell, the highest of the Pennines.

The modern county of Cumbria came into existence - or rather was resurrected - by the mandarins of Whitehall after the local government boundary changes of April 1974. Previously, the area had been split between three ancient counties which had existed for 1,000 years - Cumberland, Westmorland and Lancashire. Cumberland and Westmorland were combined, and the Whitehall bureaucrats took in the geographic anomaly of 'Lancashire-over-the Sands' to create one of the new 'super counties', and they called it Cumbria.

In doing so, they revived one of the earliest recorded names for the region. This part of north-west England had been known as Cumbraland in the Anglo-Saxon Chronicle of 945. It is a Celtic name, meaning 'the land of the Cumbrians' or Britons, and derives from the Welsh Cymry, a word which means the

Welsh, or 'foreigners' (as they were to the Saxons). Cumberland, or Cumbraland, was originally part of the British kingdom of Strathclyde, but after it was annexed by William Rufus, the name began to be used in its modern sense.

During the 5th century, after the departure of the Romans, the area now known as Cumbria had been part of a British kingdom called Rheged, which took in land on both sides of the Solway Firth; it was later incorporated into the Saxon kingdom of Northumbria, which extended on both sides of the Pennines. Westmorland was also first recorded in the Anglo-Saxon Chronicle in 966 and simply means 'the land of the Westmoringas', or the people who lived to the west of the moors of Yorkshire, while Lancashire obviously took its name from the ancient 'capital' town of that county.

The first people came late to this wild, upland region: in around 10,000 BC, as the last glaciers of the Ice Age finally relinquished their hold on the mountains of the Lake District and the Pennines, small summer parties of hunter-gatherers cautiously explored the virgin landscape in search of game and sustenance.

The original settlers in around 5,500 BC were Neolithic, or New Stone Age, people, who built the enigmatic stone circle of Castlerigg, near Keswick, at about the same time or slightly after their southern counterparts were building Stonehenge and Avebury. They established the first industry in the area with their axe 'factories', which have been found high on the slopes of the Langdale Pikes and elsewhere on the Lake District fells. They used the hard, volcanic rock to rough out their tools; these were later taken down to coastal sites for finishing and polishing, and later exported to all parts of Britain.

As the Stone Age moved into the Bronze Age, the first metal workers appeared, the only evidence of their passing being the barrows or tumuli where they buried their dead, usually cremated and left in the characteristic beakers of the Bronze Age. The Celts - or the

GRANGE-OVER-SANDS, THE PIER 1914 67426

Cymry, the first Cumbrians - followed during what is known as the Iron Age; they left behind their trademark hillforts - perhaps tribal gathering places, like those earlier stone circles - which still encircle so many hilltops in the county.

The all-conquering legions of Rome also came late to Cumbria, perhaps around AD 70, by which time the people of the area were known as the Brigantes, the tribe which dominated and ruled most of northern England from the Peak to Northumberland. The might that was Rome left many remains on the Cumbrian landscape, from the still-impressive boundary of Hadrian's Wall in the north to a network of roads and forts, such as those at Hardknott and Ambleside. Substantial settlement sites have been excavated at places like Burgh-by-Sands, Bowness-on-Solway, Maryport and Ravenglass, but this was always border country, and no prosperous villa sites have been found like those in the south of England.

The so-called 'Dark Ages' were anything but that in Cumbria, and the richness of the Celtic culture can still be seen in the magnificent carved crosses found at places like Bewcastle, Penrith and Gosforth, and the enigmatic hog-backed grave slabs found in

PENRITH, THE CHURCH 1893 32959

several churchyards like those at Penrith.

In an equally lasting way, the invading Norsemen from Ireland left a unique legacy in the language, still found in so many place-names in Cumbria. From the Old Norse tongue, they gave us the dales (from dahl), the fells (from fjall) and the tarns (from tjorn), and the first clearings they made in the forest are still known as 'thwaites' from the Old Norse thveit. That ancient language lives on in place names and dialect even today.

The Normans left their mark in the ring of castles which they built to dominate both the landscape and its people at places like Carlisle, Kendal, Cockermouth, Penrith and Egremont. But legend has it, and it seems to be borne out by the lack of any detailed reference in the Domesday Book, that they never quite subjugated the Cumbrians. The new order was more subtly introduced through the activities of the monasteries, which became enormous landowners of the fells, which were profitably managed as huge sheep ranches from places like Furness, St. Bees, Lanercost and Shap Abbeys.

As the medieval hunting forests were gradually taken in, a new breed of landowners, known as statesmen, came into being, taming the wilderness and creating the market towns of Alston, Kendal and Keswick, many of which were granted their charters during the 13th and 14th centuries. Cumbrian wool was highly valued for its durability and softness, and it clothed much of medieval Britain and Europe. The mineral riches of the fells also began to be exploited around this time, and the coal of Whitehaven, the granite of Shap, the copper ore from the Coniston fells and the iron and lead from the Pennines around Alston began to increase in importance. By the 18th and 19th centuries, Cumbria was probably better known for its industry than its scenery.

The Industrial Revolution was fired by coal and iron, and the Whitehaven and West Cumbrian coalfield had the distinct advantage of ease of transport from ready-made ports like Whitehaven and Maryport. Workington, on the mouth of the River Derwent, also became one of the major iron-smelting towns in Britain during the 18th century. By the 19th century, Barrow-in-Furness and Maryport had become two of the most important shipbuilding ports in Britain.

More than any other single figure, it was probably Cockermouth-born William Wordsworth who first 'discovered' the natural beauties of his native county, and through the ringing stanzas of his poetry, told the rest of the world about it. His 'Guide to the Lake District' of 1810 was not only the first tourist guide to the area, it was also the first recorded suggestion that the area should be set aside as 'a sort of national property, in which every man has a right and interest who has an eye to perceive and a heart to enjoy'. His words were to come true in 1951, when the Lake District became the largest of our 11 British National Parks. Wordsworth gathered around him a group of poets such as Southey, de Quincey and Coleridge who further publicised the glories of the Lake District. This has been continued by others, such as childrens' authors Beatrix Potter and Arthur Ransome, and the legendary footpath guidebook doyen Alfred Wainwright, making the Lake District one of the most popular tourist destinations in Britain with 20 million visits.

But as this book shows, there is much more to Cumbria than the Lake District, and in 1978, much of the Pennine part of Cumbria was also protected as part of the North Pennine Area of Outstanding Natural Beauty, in recognition of its natural and human heritage. This is still a quiet and largely unvisited area, as are parts of the west and north of the county.

The photographs in this book show Cumbria as it was before the tourist invasion which came in the wake of the motorcar and the motorway. They show a Cumbria which even Wordsworth and Coleridge might have recognised.

Chapter One: The Lakes

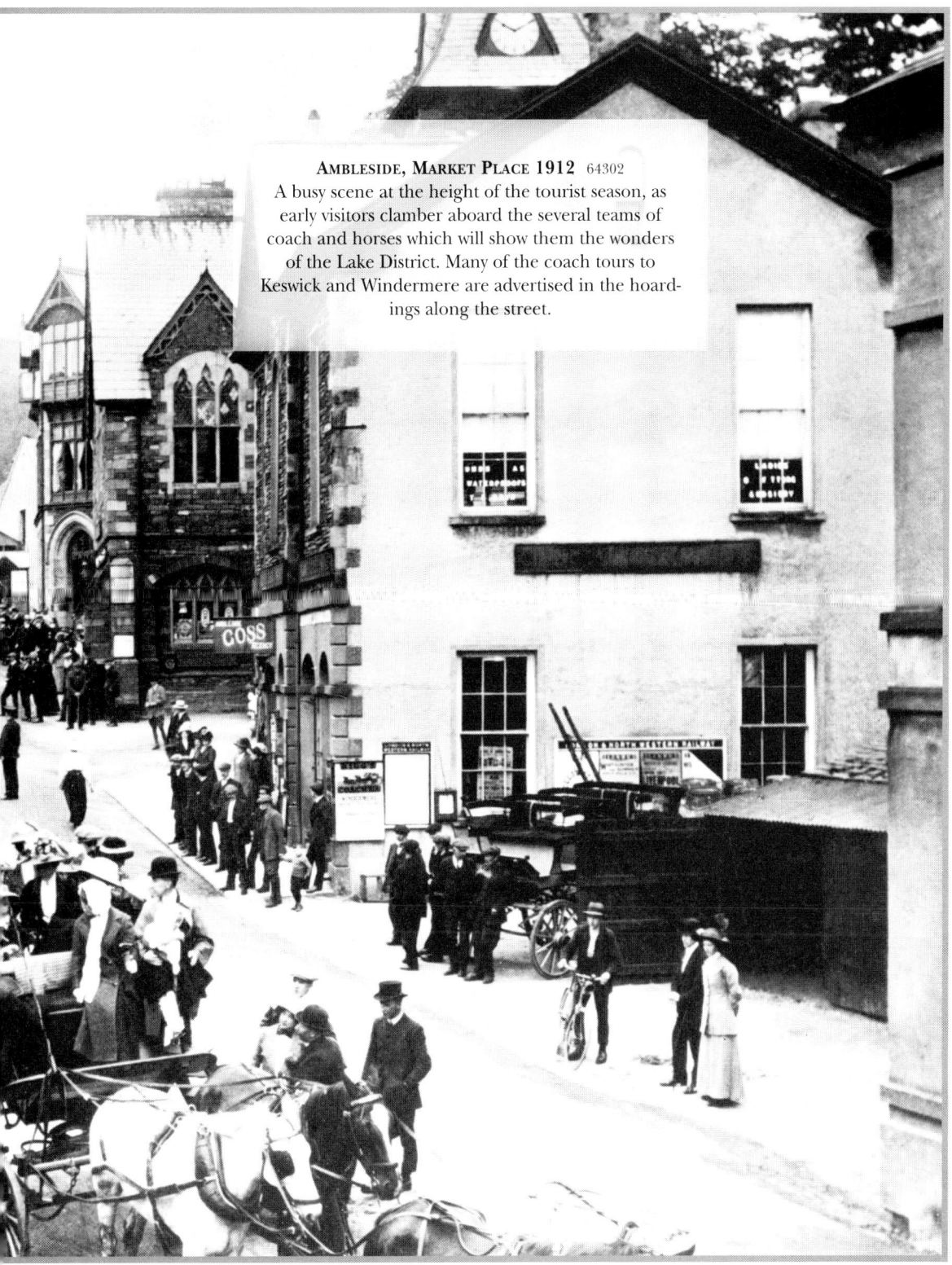

AMBLESIDE, MARKET PLACE 1912 64302
A busy scene at the height of the tourist season, as early visitors clamber aboard the several teams of coach and horses which will show them the wonders of the Lake District. Many of the coach tours to Keswick and Windermere are advertised in the hoardings along the street.

Francis Frith's Cumbria

AMBLESIDE, MARKET PLACE 1927 79174
This photograph, looking south from the Market Place in the opposite direction from photograph No 64302, and taken 15 years later, shows a very different scene. The street is almost deserted apart from a motor lorry, motorcycle and a few pedestrians, showing that the photograph was probably taken in the winter, outside the tourist season.

The Lakes

AMBLESIDE, WATERHEAD FERRY 1912 64321

AMBLESIDE
Waterhead Ferry 1912
A crowded WSV 'Tern' prepares to embark on a trip down Windermere from the Waterhead pier on a summer's day. The Edwardian costumes of the passengers are interesting to note - the ladies are all wearing the large hats and long dresses of the time, while most of the men sport straw hats or bowlers.

◆

AMBLESIDE
Stock Ghyll Force 1886
The waterfalls of Stock Ghyll Force have been a major attraction to visitors to Ambleside for well over a century, but this is a very early photograph of them. The waters of Stock Ghyll rise just below the summit of the Kirkstone Pass, north of the town, and plunge through this wooded gorge before joining the River Rothay and eventually entering Windermere.

AMBLESIDE, STOCK GHYLL FORCE 1886 18686

AMBLESIDE, SWEDEN BRIDGE 1912 64330D

AMBLESIDE
Sweden Bridge 1912
High Sweden Bridge is a picturesque packhorse bridge over the Scandale Beck between High Pike and Snarker Pike (there is a Low Sweden Bridge lower down the valley). It has no direct Scandinavian connection, other than the fact that the name comes from the Norse 'svithinn' and means 'land cleared by burning'.

AMBLESIDE
Tarn Hows c1955
A classic view of Tarn Hows, near Hawkshead, with the peaks of the Langdale Pikes in the centre background. Despite its natural appearance, the lakes of Tarn Hows are in fact artificial, and there were once several smaller tarns. About 80 years ago, the landowner dammed the beck to create this familiar scene - one of the most visited places in the Lake District.

AMBLESIDE, TARN HOWS c1955 A46145

The Lakes

BOWNESS, ST MARTIN'S SQUARE 1955 B166012
St. Martin's Square takes its name from the nearby parish church, which was consecrated in 1483 and contains medieval glass which is thought to come from Cartmel Priory. The church was enlarged to its present form in 1870, and it watches over the older part of Bowness, which is known as Lowside.

BOWNESS, THE PIER 1887 20451
A smartly-painted Windermere steamer sets out, with the Old England Hotel, one of many which sprang up in this little town as tourism took hold in the Lake District at the turn of the 19th century, in the background.

BOWNESS, THE BOAT STATION AND THE OLD ENGLAND HOTEL 1893 31938
There are plenty of rowing boats for visitors at the Bowness Boat Station in this photograph, taken just six years after No 20451. The ivy-covered Old England Hotel in the background has not changed significantly.

BOWNESS, THE FERRY BOAT 1887 20462
The Bowness Ferry across the narrowest part of Windermere was originally a rowing boat, but it became steam-operated just 17 years before this photograph was taken. On board for the short trip to the western shore at Sawrey are two horses and carts.

The Lakes

BOWNESS
The Ferry arriving at the Nab c1955
By the time this photograph was taken, cars had replaced the horses and carts, and the crossing was accomplished by a chain-operated pulley. The wooded Claife Heights on the western shore are prominent in the background.

◆

BORROWDALE
Grange 1893
The hamlet of Grange-in-Borrowdale was originally founded as an outlying settlement from the medieval monastery of Furness Abbey. Still a tiny hamlet, situated where the River Derwent meanders through water meadows to join Derwent Water to the north, it is a popular centre for fell walkers. The peak of High Spy is in the background.

BOWNESS, THE FERRY ARRIVING AT THE NAB c1955 B166017

BORROWDALE, GRANGE 1893 32886

BORROWDALE, THE HOTEL 1870 5047
This very early postcard view of the Borrowdale Hotel, with Grange Crags behind, shows the Lake District as it was before the tourist invasion really took hold. The traffic-free minor road meanders south between drystone walls through the dale, towards Grange and Rosthwaite.

BUTTERMERE, HAYMAKING c1955 B260064
Agriculture in the 1950s had not changed much since the 19th century, and horses were still commonly used on the land. This scene showing the loading of a hay wagon on the shores of Buttermere, with Honister Crag and Fleetwith Pike prominent in the background, shows that timeless way of life.

The Lakes

CRUMMOCK WATER 1893 32907
This scene, looking from the head of Crummock Water towards Buttermere with Honister Crag, Fleetwith Pike, Haystacks and High Stile forming the mountainous background, has hardly changed in a century. The twin lakes of Crummock Water and Buttermere were once one, but were separated by the alluvium left by Sail Beck.

CONISTON, THE 'GONDOLA' PIER 1906 54243
The famous steam cruiser the 'Gondola' is seen here tied up and waiting for passengers at the Waterhead Pier on Coniston Water. The Gondola was built in 1859 to take tourists up and down the lake, but was later neglected and became a rotting hulk before being restored in 1980 by its present owners, the National Trust.

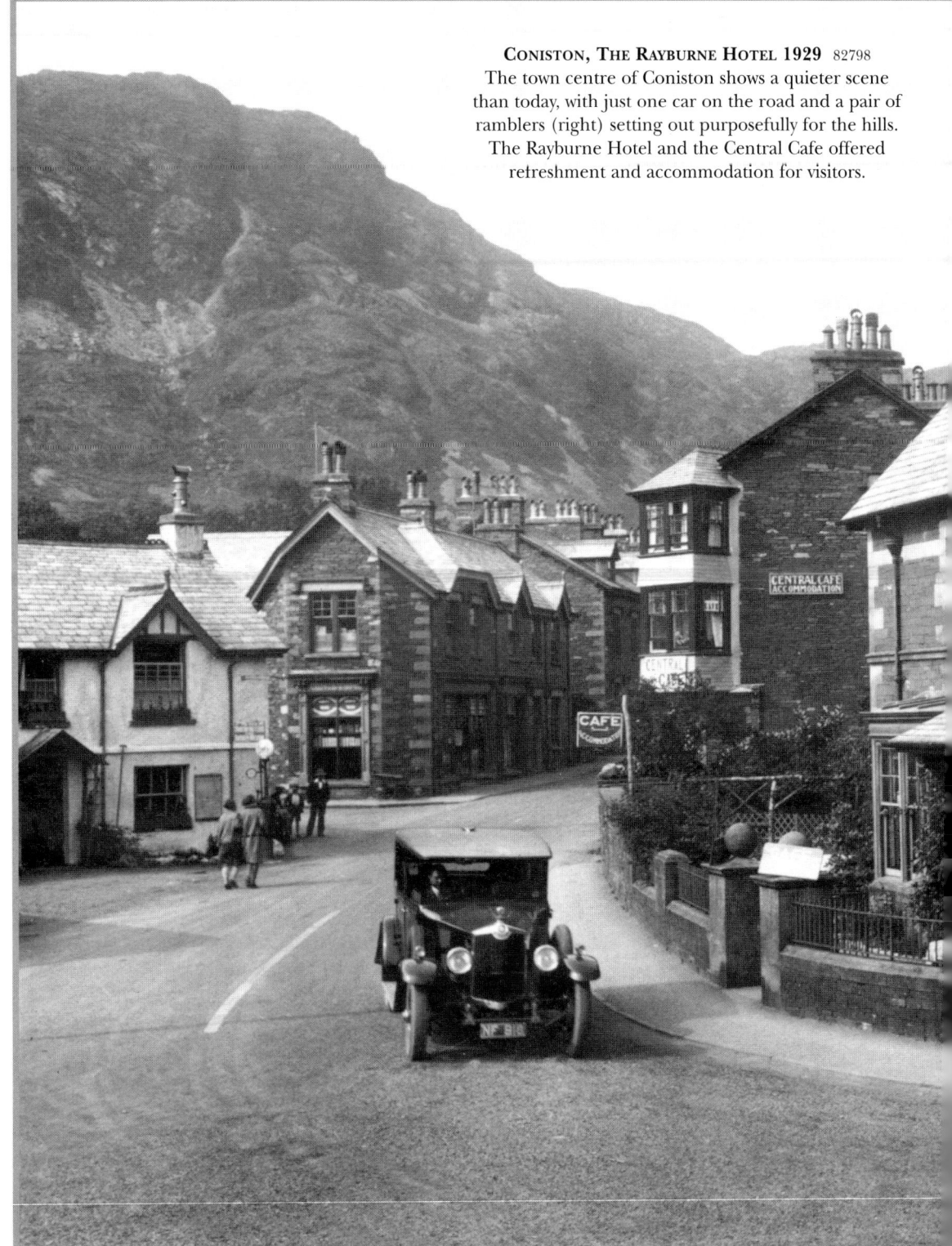

CONISTON, THE RAYBURNE HOTEL 1929 82798
The town centre of Coniston shows a quieter scene than today, with just one car on the road and a pair of ramblers (right) setting out purposefully for the hills. The Rayburne Hotel and the Central Cafe offered refreshment and accommodation for visitors.

The Lakes

CONISTON, THE FELLS 1912 64276
A horse and cart wends its way up a gated minor road through the Coniston Fells. At the time before the coming of the motor car in significant numbers, there were many roads like this in the Lake District, and life continued among the hills at the same leisurely pace as it had for centuries.

DERWENT WATER, FRIAR'S CRAG 1893 32862
Another classic view of the Lake District. The pine-clad promontory of Friar's Crag near Keswick on Derwent Water is backed by the forested slopes of Walla Crag. Friar's Crag obtained its name as the embarkation point for monks crossing to St Herbert's Island.

The Lakes

DERWENT WATER, THE LODORE HOTEL 1893 32878
Shepherd's Crag towers through the trees over the Victorian Gothic buildings of the Lodore Hotel at the southern end of Derwent Water. Just behind the hotel, also in the trees, are the twin cascades of Lodore Falls, a popular sight for visitors in Victorian days.

DERWENT WATER AND ASHNESS BRIDGE 1893 32871
The tiny hump-backed bridge at Ashness on the narrow road which leads up from the eastern shore of Derwent Water to the Norse hamlet of Watendlath has been seen on countless Lake District calendars, but this must be one of the earliest photographs. The bold profile of Skiddaw fills the background across the lake.

GRASMERE, THE CHURCH 1926 79209
Now the centre of a hectic one-way traffic system, Grasmere's parish church of St Oswald is perhaps best known for being the last resting place of the poet William Wordsworth, who is buried there alongside his wife, Mary, and sister and constant companion, Dorothy. Things were much quieter when this photograph was taken.

GRASMERE, RED LION SQUARE 1926 79207
Red Lion Square takes its name from the famous old inn on the left of this photograph. It is surrounded by the simple grey slate-gabled shops and houses which are so typical of a small Lake District town.

The Lakes

GRASMERE
The Swan Hotel 1926
The Swan Hotel stands on the outskirts of the village of Grasmere, on the A591, and was formerly a coaching inn on the main road between Windermere and Keswick. Like many Lake District inns, it was painted white to keep it weatherproof.

HELVELLYN
Striding Edge 1912
The glaciated knife-edge ridge of Striding Edge was already a popular route of ascent to 3,118 ft Helvellyn when this photograph was taken, if the prominence of the path along its crest is anything to go by. This view is from the summit, looking east towards High Spying How.

GRASMERE, THE SWAN HOTEL 1926 79203

HELVELLYN, STRIDING EDGE 1912 64344

Francis Frith's Cumbria

HAWKSHEAD, MARKET SQUARE 1929 82372
A holidaying family relax with their dog outside the Old King's Arms pub and boarding house in the cobbled centre of the ancient village of Hawkshead. Now that the village has been by-passed, some of the serenity of this photograph has returned to Hawkshead, although today it is seldom as quiet as this.

The Lakes

HAWKSHEAD, MARKET SQUARE 1929 82367
Another view of Market Square, with the ivy-clad building of Wilson's High Class Confectioners and the Esthwaite Cafe in the centre of the photograph, and the King's Arms in the background. Local children play unconcerned by traffic in the middle of the street.

HAWKSHEAD, MAIN STREET AND THE POST OFFICE 1912 64292
The popularity of Frith's postcards was already well established when this photograph was taken, as a sign on the wall above the door shows. They may well be Frith's postcards displayed on the boards outside the shop. Note the jettied buildings opposite, typical of Hawkshead.

The Lakes

HAWKSHEAD, THE GRAMMAR SCHOOL 1892 30538
William Wordsworth must have looked out from these mullioned windows of the ancient Grammar School, where he was educated between 1779 and 1787. The school, now a museum and library, sits comfortably beneath the bank on which the parish church of St. Michael, seen in the background, stands.

KENDAL, STRAMONGATE BRIDGE 1891 28619
Stramongate Bridge was also known as Miller or Mill Bridge, because it linked the mills on the eastern bank of the River Kent to the 'Auld Grey Town' on the other bank. Stramongate is the main approach road into Kendal from the north-east, and means 'the street of the straw men'. St. George's Church is in the background.

Francis Frith's Cumbria

KENDAL, THE COUNTY HOTEL 1924 75801
The County Hotel is one of the main hotels in the centre of Kendal and dominates this part of the old town, whose wealth was founded on the woollen and textile industries. The famed Kendal bowmen at the Battle of Flodden Field (1513) were clad in home-spun Kendal Green cloth.

The Lakes

Kendal
St. George's Church and the Weir 1891
The twin Italianate towers of St. George's Church dominate this view of Kendal, across the River Kent and its weir. The river has always been important for Kendal, and powered many of the mills which wove the famous Kendal Green and other textiles from the Middle Ages onwards. It is perhaps best known now for the delicious Kendal Mint Cake.

◆

Kendal
The Parish Church 1914
Kendal's church of the Holy Trinity is Cumbria's largest parish church, and dates from the 13th century, although it was extensively restored 60 years before this photograph was taken, between 1850 and 1852. It has five aisles, two on each side of the nave and chancel, and a fine tower with a peal of 10 bells.

KENDAL, ST. GEORGE'S CHURCH AND THE WEIR 1891 28620

KENDAL, THE CHURCH 1914 67374

The Lakes

KENDAL, THE GRAMMAR SCHOOL 1891 28622

KENDAL
The Grammar School 1891
The Grammar School was newly-completed when this photograph was taken. Kendal has always been an important service centre for the southern Lake District, and today is the headquarters of both the South Lakeland District Council and the Lake District National Park Authority.

◆

KENDAL
An Old Yard off Stricklandgate 1914
One of the most engaging characteristics of Kendal is its multitude of charming side alleys and yards, such as this off the main thoroughfare of Stricklandgate. This is an old name which means 'the road leading to the stirk (cattle) land' and refers to the use of the road to drive cattle into market from the north.

KENDAL, AN OLD YARD OFF STRICKLANDGATE 1914 67398

KENDAL, THE CASTLE 1896 38538
Kendal Castle, originally a 13th-century structure, was owned by the family of Katherine Parr, the last wife of Henry VIII, in the 16th century. At that time the castle was in the hands of Sir Thomas Parr. This view shows the exterior of the main hall, the most impressive of the ruins left, and now the centre of a public park.

KENDAL, LEVENS HALL 1891 28630
The gardens and the topiary at Levens Hall, near Kendal, were laid out by the King's gardener, Beaumont, in 1692. Beaumont trained at Versailles and was in much demand, but spent the last 40 years of his life working for James Bellingham at Levens Hall. This beautiful Elizabethan manor house is now the home of the Bagot family.

The Lakes

KESWICK, GENERAL VIEW 1886 6755
The smooth slopes of 3,054-ft Skiddaw dominates the northern Lakeland town of Keswick in this view from Castle Head. The 19th century parish church of St John is prominent in the centre of the picture, while the rest of the town spreads out beneath Skiddaw (right) and Dodd on the left.

KESWICK, THE DRUID STONES 1889 22090
The Castlerigg Stone Circle just outside Keswick was still erroneously being called the Druid Stones when this photograph was taken. Actually, this impressive stone circle dates from the Neolithic or early Bronze Age period, and predates the Celtic Druids by many centuries. The mistake was repeated by the poet John Keats, who referred to the stones as 'a dismal cirque of Druid stones upon a forlorn moor'.

LANGDALE PIKES 1892 30515
An extensive view down the valley of Great Langdale, with Harrison Stickle (2,403ft) and Gimmer Crag prominent on the skyline. At this time, the great mountains of the Lake District were just being 'discovered' by climbers such as the Abraham Brothers of Keswick, O G Jones and Walter Parry Haskett Smith.

The Lakes

Francis Frith's Cumbria

LANGDALE PIKES, THE MOUNTAIN 1888 20507
Another view of Harrison Stickle, highest of the Langdale Pikes, this time from the valley at the bridge near the Dungeon Ghyll Hotel, a favourite haunt of walkers and climbers. Stickle Ghyll flows down from Stickle Tarn and under the bridge.

NEWBY BRIDGE, GENERAL VIEW 1914 67411
Two lads enjoy the view from the hillside above Newby Bridge, the small village at the southern end of Windermere, with the low south Lakeland hills in the background. The village takes its name from the bridge, visible in the middle distance of the photograph, which crosses the River Leven here.

The Lakes

NEWBY BRIDGE, THE BRIDGE 1914 67415
A family picnic by the five-arched bridge originally built in the 16th century over the River Leven. Note the then-fashionable straw hats, and the wrought iron frame protecting the wooden signpost by the lady on the left.

TROUTBECK, THE VALLEY c1880 12523
The Troutbeck valley is one of the quietest in the Lake District, and in this view, taken from the old coach route between Windermere and Penrith, the essentially rural nature of much of the district can still be appreciated. The white-painted farmhouse in the valley was probably occupied by one of the district's famous 'statesmen' farmers.

WINDERMERE, VICTORIA STREET 1929 82818
There is not much traffic in Victoria Street at this time. Victoria Street leads off Church Street, now the A591, in this busy little town which was originally known as Birthwaite, but changed its name to match that of the nearby lake when the railway arrived in 1847.

The Lakes

Chapter Two: North Cumbria

Abbeytown, Main Street c1965 A286002
It is ten past twelve on a summer's afternoon in the mid-sixties in this sleepy North Cumbrian town - and there is not a vehicle in sight in the length of the long Main Street. Abbeytown takes its name from the 12th-century Holme Cultram Abbey, parts of which are incorporated in the parish church of St Mary.

Armathwaite, The Red Lion Hotel c1965 A293016
The Red Lion Hotel in the charming village of Armathwaite occupies a beautiful position at the foot of a tree-clad bank above the River Eden. Its name is thought to mean 'the clearing of the hermit', and it is perhaps best known today as a stop on the famous trans-Pennine Settle to Carlisle railway.

North Cumbria

ASPATRIA, MARKET PLACE C1960 A295006
The memorial fountain to Sir Wilfred Lawrence, the local MP and campaigner in the Temperance Movement, dominates the Market Place. Aspatria's unusual-sounding name means 'the place of St. Patrick's ash', a reference to the early Celtic Christians who followed the Irish saint.

BAMPTON GRANGE, THE VILLAGE 1952 B299005
The parish church of St Patrick, in the background, is only one of ten in England dedicated to Ireland's patron saint. It underlines the persistent local tradition that St Patrick visited this part of the Lowther Valley.

Francis Frith's Cumbria

BRAMPTON, MARKET PLACE C1955 B520002
The sloping Market Place leads up to the white-painted clock tower of the town's octagonal Moot Hall, which was built in 1817. Unusually, the Moot Hall has an external staircase to its first floor entrance, like that of the Old Town Hall in nearby Carlisle.

North Cumbria

BRAMPTON, NAWORTH CASTLE c1955 B520006
Naworth Castle, about two miles east of Brampton, is the family home of the Howards, Earls of Carlisle. It was an old Border stronghold, the oldest part of which is the Dacre Tower, an old pele tower, which dates from the 14th century. Lord William Howard, 'Belted Will', converted it to a mansion in the 17th century, and it was later damaged by fire before being restored in the 19th century.

BROUGHAM CASTLE 1893 32938
Brougham Castle, a red sandstone pile on the River Eamont, two miles south-east of Penrith, was the last resting place of the legendary Lady Anne Clifford, Countess of Dorset. She made improvements to the originally Norman building, which was strengthened by Henry II in 1170.

North Cumbria

BURGH-BY-SANDS, THE RAILWAY STATION c1955 B709004
Neatly-kept gardens and colourful flowerbeds brighten the station buildings at Burgh-by-Sands, a small village near the mouth of the Eden on the Solway Firth. Burgh was also close to the western end of Hadrian's Wall, and the parish church of St Michael is built within a Roman fort.

CARLISLE, MARKET PLACE c1935 C211001
Carlisle's spacious Market Place is now completely pedestrianised. But the long, low, whitewashed shape of the Old Town Hall on the left is still recognisable, although it is now a Tourist Information Centre. The fine sandstone buildings which line the streets which surround the Market still impart the sense of importance of this fine city, for so long a pivotal Border stronghold.

North Cumbria

GREYSTOKE, THE CASTLE 1893 32957
Greystoke Castle was built around a 14th-century pele tower in the Tudor style between 1838 and 1848 for the locally-powerful Greystoke family. The architect was Anthony Salvin. His services were called on once again in 1868, when the house caught fire and several works of art and other treasures were lost. For this later work he employed the estate craftsmen and used only local materials.

North Cumbria

GREYSTOKE, THE CASTLE 1893 32956
In the Second World War the castle was requisitioned by the military for the training of tank drivers. It was not until 1950 that Stafford Howard took control once again on behalf of the family. The castle stands at the centre of a neat estate type village, which is perhaps best known for champion jockey Sir Gordon Richards' racing stables.

LANERCOST PRIORY, THE CHURCH 1924 76666
The red sandstone ruins of Lanercost Priory stand above the River Irthing near Brampton. The priory was founded in 1166 for the Augustinian Order, and building continued for about 50 years, constantly interrupted by raids by Scots. The nave of the priory is now the parish church for the tiny village, and is dedicated to St Mary

MARYPORT, SENHOUSE STREET c1955 M262015
The basket of a grocery delivery cycle is prominent on the extreme left. The name of this busy shopping street is significant because it commemorates Lord of the Manor Colonel Humphrey Senhouse, who expanded the town greatly in the 18th century, and renamed it after his wife, Mary.

North Cumbria

MARYPORT, THE HARBOUR c1955 M262016
Low tide in the harbour, which was another of the creations of Colonel Senhouse in the mid 18th century. In its heyday, the port would be filled with up to 80 vessels, exporting the locally mined coal and iron ore, but today it is largely silted up and used only for small fishing boats and weekend sailors.

LONGTOWN, HIGH STREET c1955 L203004
A virtually deserted tree-lined High Street in Longtown, a small town on the Esk a few miles short of the Scottish Border. Locals gather outside the Globe Tavern, perhaps waiting for opening time. Longtown has mythical connections with King Arthur, and still stands in the parish of Arthuret.

North Cumbria

GREYSTOKE, THE CHURCH 1893 32959
Greystoke Church dates from 13th century. Chantries were added to the original structure by the 14th Baron Greystoke, who built the first Greystoke Castle. These had painted oak screens, which were removed during the Reformation, giving the nave a broader and more expansive appearance. The tower was used as a pele tower by villagers, who hid there from marauding Scots.

PENRITH
Wordsworth Street 1893 32931A
Penrith, 'capital' of the northern Lake District, is an attractive
red sandstone market town. But it did not escape the 'Poets'
Corner' craze for street-naming of the late 19th century. At least
Penrith's Wordsworth Street, had a genuine claim to the
local poet.

North Cumbria

PENRITH
Lowther Lodge 1893

Here we see the lodge to Lowther Castle. Lowther Castle was built between 1806 and 1811 by the 1st Earl of Lonsdale to a Gothic design by Robert Smirke, who later designed the British Museum. The Lowther family later abandoned the castle, and it is now a wildlife park.

◆

PENRITH
Askham Bridge 1893 32945

Askham, four miles south of Penrith, is one of the most attractive villages in the former county of Westmorland, and Askham Bridge, spanning the River Lowther, is one of the most graceful structures. This scene, with its rocky riverbed and tree-clad banks, has hardly changed in a century.

PENRITH, LOWTHER LODGE 1893 32937

PENRITH, ASKHAM BRIDGE 1893 32945

SILLOTH, CRIFFEL STREET c1955 S658001
Tree-lined Criffel Street, in the handsome Solway seaside town of Silloth, is a reminder of the proximity of the Scottish Border. The peak of Criffel in Dumfries can easily be seen across the Solway Firth from the stony beach-front. The spire of the parish church of Christ Church punctuates this photograph.

WETHERAL, THE ROAD TO THE RIVER c1955 W497017
A family party makes its way down to the River Eden on a hot summer's day. Wetheral congregates around its spacious triangular village green, which is overlooked by a number of fine, large 18th-century houses.

North Cumbria

WIGTON, THE SQUARE c1965 W424033
The fountain in the centre of Wigton's Square or Market Place has a pyramidal cross-topped spire, and depicted on its four sides are the four Acts of Mercy. Wigton is a pleasant market town with much good Georgian architecture, lying in the broad fertile Solway Plain.

WIGTON, KING STREET c1955 W424018
The union flags are out: perhaps the local people were celebrating the Coronation of Queen Elizabeth. The scene has not changed much today, other than the inevitable increase in the volume of traffic through this delightful Cumbrian market town.

Chapter Three: The Cumbrian Pennines

Alston, Market Cross c1955 A290055
Claimed to be the highest market town in England, Alston commands sweeping views of the North Pennines and the South Tyne Valley. This charming little town clusters around its cobbled, sloping Market Place. The parish church of St Augustine, in the background of this picture, was extensively rebuilt in Victorian times.

Alston, Front Street c1955 A290011
Cobbled Front Street slopes steeply down towards the South Tyne Valley, past 17th-century cottages, like that on the extreme right which is dated 1681, and ancient pubs like the Angel and the King's Arms, further down the street.

The Cumbrian Pennines

BARBON, THE VILLAGE 1901 47027
The pretty little village of Barbon, near Kirkby Lonsdale, lies in the hills above the Lune Valley beneath Thorn Moor, on the minor road through Barbondale to Dent. If there ever was a village which time passed by, this is it, and it has changed little since this photograph was taken.

BROUGH, THE VILLAGE c1955 B604002
Originally there were three Broughs, and this view shows what is properly known as Market Brough. Church Brough is clustered around the parish church of St Michael, and there is also an area of the town known as Brough Sowerby. The Market Cross shown here marks the site of the market which grew up around the 14th-century bridge which crosses Swindale Beck.

COLDBECK
The Old Smithy c1955

By the time when this picture was taken, Coldbeck's Old Smithy had already been converted to a gift shop. The village is on the Scandale Beck near Ravenstonedale on the northern flanks of the Howgill Fells, in an area rich in prehistory and mercifully bypassed by the A685 road to Kirkby Stephen.

◆

COLDBECK
Sheep Shearing c1955

This scene on a Coldbeck farm has not changed for centuries. As the hand on the right shears a Swaledale sheep watched by two lads, his mates to the left fold the fleeces in the time-honoured way, ready for selling.

COLDBECK, THE OLD SMITHY c1955 C567029

COLDBECK, SHEEP SHEARING c1955 C567031

The Cumbrian Pennines

DENT, MAIN STREET 1924 75624
The cobbled Main Street, with The Sun Inn at the top of the street, remains very much the same today. The village postman poses for the photographer, while another villager gets a bucket of water from the fountain memorial to Dent's most famous son, the pioneer geologist Adam Sedgwick. This was long before tapped water supplies had reached this remote village.

DENT, MAIN STREET 1924 75625
This view looks in the opposite direction from photograph No 75624. This time, two children are filling their bucket from the fountain, and the George and Dragon Hotel, which welcomed members of the Cyclists' Touring Club, is the prominent building on the right.

GARRIGILL, THE GREEN c1955 G259009
Garrigill is a typical North Pennine village, clustered defensively around its central green in which stock would be gathered in time of attack. The village stands on the River South Tyne, not far from its source and just below Cross Fell, at 2,930ft the highest summit in the Pennines.

KIRKBY LONSDALE, MARKET SQUARE 1908 59539
Local tradesmen pose for the cameraman in front of the ornate octagonal open Market Cross in the Market Place, centrepiece of this lovely little town which many people believe to be the most beautiful in the old county of Westmorland. In the background, under its handsome pedimented clock, is the local Savings Bank.

The Cumbrian Pennines

KIRKBY LONSDALE, MARKET PLACE 1926 79102
Another view of Kirkby's Market Place taken nearly 20 years after photograph No 59539, and showing few changes apart from the motor vehicles; these include the charabanc which plied between Lancaster and Sedburgh, parked by the Market Cross. The Waverley Cafe, opposite the Cross, advertises Lune Salmon Teas, no doubt freshly caught from the local river.

KIRKBY LONSDALE, THE ROYAL HOTEL 1899 42878
This view looks in the opposite direction from photograph No 79102, from outside the Royal Hotel (left). This was originally known as the Rose and Crown, but changed its name in 1840 after the Dowager Queen Adelaide, widow of William IV, convalesced here while touring in the north of England in that year.

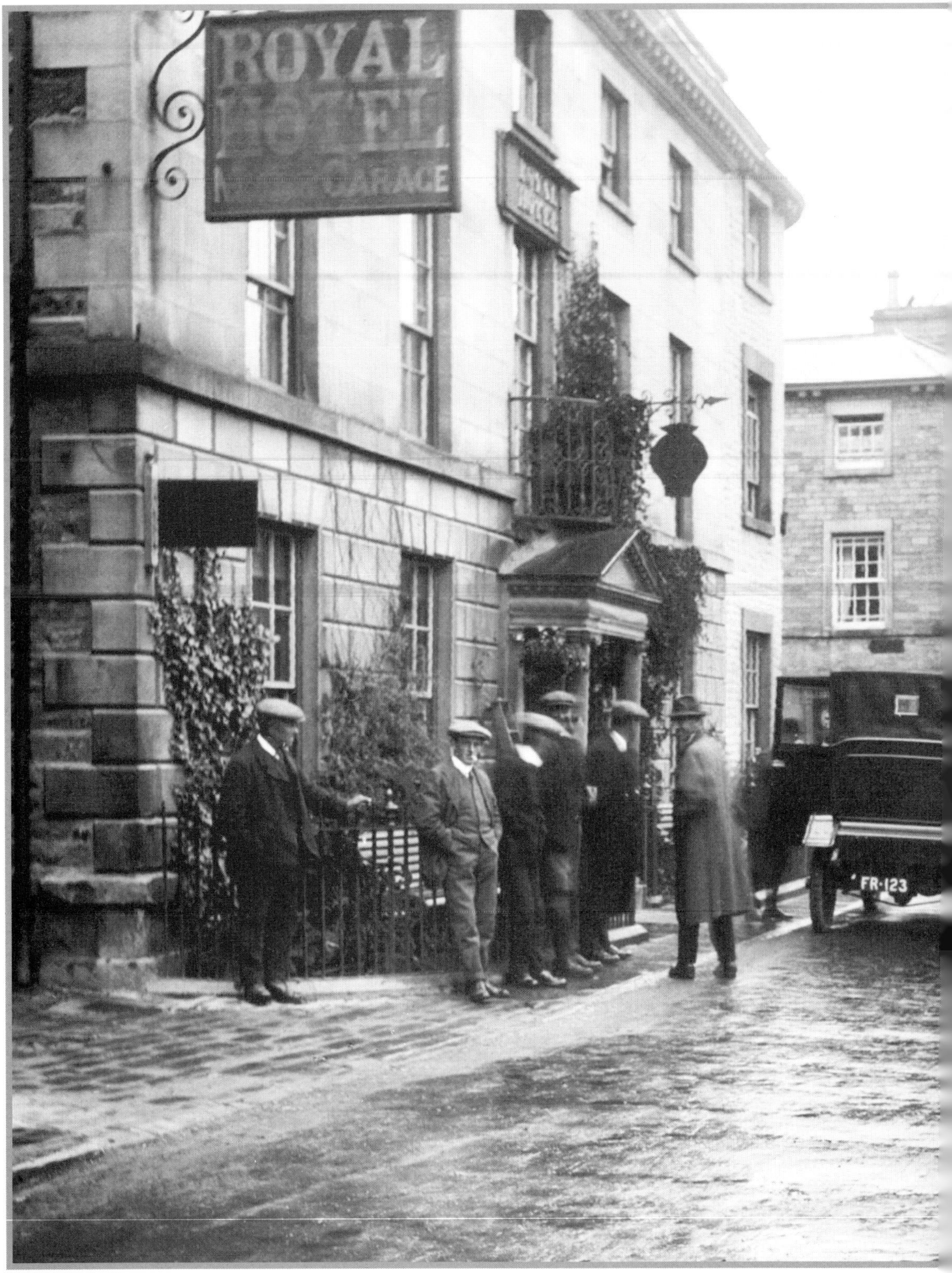
ROYAL
FR-123

The Cumbrian Pennines

KIRKBY LONSDALE, THE ROYAL HOTEL 1914 67344
The same scene as photograph No 42878, 15 years later, shows a virtually unchanged scene, but with a motor car parked outside the hotel, which no longer seems to cater for Cyclist Touring Club members as it did in 1899. Cloth-capped local men, hands in pockets, wait outside the hotel in the rain, perhaps waiting for transport themselves.

Francis Frith's Cumbria

Kirkby Lonsdale, Main Street 1908 59555
This is the scene looking back down Kirkby's Main Street towards the Royal Hotel, which can just be seen in the distance. The rather odd looking and out-of-scale motor car in the centre of the road has been transplanted from another photograph - a common practice in the early days, used to prolong the life of a postcard.

Kirkby Lonsdale, Main Street 1908 59554
This view was taken from virtually the same spot as photograph No 59555, looking in the opposite direction. Local children, clad in the long dresses and knickerbocker trousers of Edwardian times, stare inquisitively at the camera - the lads on the right ready with bat and ball for a game of cricket. Note the jettied shop front on the left.

The Cumbrian Pennines

KIRKBY LONSDALE, DEVIL'S BRIDGE 1899 42874
Kirkby Lonsdale's famous Devil's Bridge over the River Lune traditionally gets its name because it was built by the Devil, who claimed the soul of the first being to cross it. In the event, it was nothing more than an old dog. In fact, the elegant, soaring structure was probably first built in the 12th century.

KIRKBY STEPHEN, MARKET STREET c1960 K148015
The town was granted its right to hold a market during the 14th century, and bull-baiting was carried out in the Market Square until 1840. There are some fine Georgian buildings along Market Street, including the Black Bull Hotel, on the left.

Francis Frith's Cumbria

LAZONBY, FROM THE CHURCH TOWER c1955 L346002
The view across the village from the tower of the parish church of St. Nicholas. This hilltop village above the River Eden grew in importance after the coming of the railway in 1876; it is perhaps best known for the red sandstone which was quarried from nearby Lazonby Fell and used in the construction of Liverpool's Anglican Cathedral.

MORLAND, THE VILLAGE 1893 32964
A local character lounges on a wall on the left in the charming and unspoilt village of Morland, in the Eden Valley. A horse and cart can be seen in the far distance, while the footbridge on the right crosses the Morland Beck, which once powered several small mills in the village.

The Cumbrian Pennines

SEDBERGH, MARKET PLACE 1894 34078
Sedbergh is a pleasant little market town on the southern edge of the lovely Howgill Fells. Two men converse outside a hardware store on the left, while the Bull Hotel, seen in photograph No 46914, can be seen at the far end of the street.

SEDBERGH, MAIN STREET 1901 46914
The tightly-packed shops in Sedbergh's Main Street have not changed much since this photograph was taken. Note the goods piled outside on the pavement outside Jackson's hardware store on the right, and the horse and cart further down the street. The Bull Hotel in the centre of the picture is still described as a 'Posting House'.

SEDBERGH, MARKET PLACE 1901 46913
The bold black-and-white half-timbering of G Sedgwick's draper and outfitters shop in the centre of the picture (the owners are proudly standing outside) is in marked contrast to the same shop which can be seen sticking out into the street in photograph No 34078. On the left, a coach and handcart are unceremoniously parked on the corner of Finkle Street.

SEDBERGH MARKET PLACE 1894 34077
Here the Market Place has a fair number of local people and tradesmen curiously watching the cameraman's antics in the middle of the street. On the left is the 1858 Market Hall, with a milk carter's wagon outside, complete with milk churn. The shop on the right is insured with the West of England Fire and Life Insurance Company.

Chapter Four: South Cumbria

ALLITHWAITE
Kirkhead Tower c1965
The folly of Kirkhead Tower stands on a headland overlooking the small coastal village of Allithwaite, which takes its name from a Norse settler named Eilifr. To the south lies Humphrey Head, which according to legend was the place where the last wolf in England was killed.

◆

ARNSIDE
The Beach 1894
Two youngsters are digging for shrimps in the sands of the beach at Arnside, where the River Kent enters Morecambe Bay, while in the background three adults sit on the seawall. Arnside became a popular seaside resort in the 19th century, when pleasure boats would come up from Morecambe and Fleetwood.

ALLITHWAITE, KIRKHEAD TOWER C1965 A288003

ARNSIDE, THE BEACH 1894 34130

Francis Frith's Cumbria

ARNSIDE, FROM THE BEACH 1894 34128
Here a little Victorian girl poses among the rowing boats laid up on the beach at Arnside. Once a thriving port and Westmorland's only link to the sea, Arnside eventually lost its trade to better placed harbours.

ARNSIDE, THE TOWER AND THE KNOTT 1894 34134
Arnside Tower is a large, ruinous pele tower built during the 15th century as a protection against marauding Scots. It was badly damaged by fire in 1602, but still watches over the Kent Estuary beneath the limestone mass of Arnside Knott, seen here rising to the left of the picture.

South Cumbria

BARDSEA, THE STORES c1930 B20012
A family pose for the photographer outside the village stores in the tiny hamlet of Bardsea on the northern shores of Morecambe Bay. Bardsea was a fishing hamlet at the time, serving a small community of shrimpers and farmers.

BARDSEA, THE LANDING PLACE c1930 B20015
At one time, Bardsea was part of Lancashire, and could only be reached by boat or by a dangerous route over the shifting sands of Morecambe Bay from Lancaster. This small harbour was once used to unload coal and take on iron ore and corn from the surrounding countryside.

Francis Frith's Cumbria

BARDSEA, THE BARDSEA BOAT c1930 B20016
Passengers on the beach at Bardsea await the raising of the mast in the large sailing boat which will take them down the coast at high tide. Bardsea was also a popular port of call for sailing boats from Morecambe and Fleetwood.

BARDSEA, THE BEACH 1895 35913
A family of youngsters enjoy a spot of shrimping on the beach. On the skyline in the background is the parish church of the Holy Trinity, consecrated just 40 years earlier in 1853.

South Cumbria

BARROW-IN-FURNESS, DUKE STREET 1893 32988
Note the handcarts parked at the side of the street on the right, and the advertising hoardings on the side of the shop on the left of the picture, advertising among other things 'Wheatleys Hop Bitters'.

BARROW-IN-FURNESS, DUKE STREET 1898 41428
Note the tramlines in the street, and the industrial chimney on the left. The horse-drawn carts are parked outside the photographic shop of Hollis Wilkins, which advertises 'Life-sized Heads, Direct from Life'.

BARROW-IN-FURNESS, DALTON ROAD 1912 64405
Pedestrians could walk down the middle of the street with impunity when this mid-morning photograph was taken just before the First World War. And photography was still so unusual that the camera turned more than a few heads among the Edwardian population.

South Cumbria

Francis Frith's Cumbria

BARROW-IN-FURNESS, WALNEY BRIDGE 1912 64407
Shipbuilders swarm across the Walney Bridge from the dockyards at the end of a working day. A crane at Vickers dockyard can be seen in the background on the right. Protected by the enclosing reef of Walney Island, Barrow flourished as a major shipbuilding centre in the 19th and early 20th centuries.

South Cumbria

BARROW-IN-FURNESS, THE ABBEY 1892 30574
The red sandstone walls of Furness Abbey were built in the 12th century, started under the Savigny Order by Stephen, Count of Boulogne, later King of England. It later became a part of the Cistercian empire, second only in importance and wealth to Fountains Abbey in the Yorkshire Dales.

BARROW-IN-FURNESS, THE ABBEY 1892 30570
This view shows the late Norman arches of the cloisters. After the Dissolution of the Monasteries (1536-9) it became the property of Thomas Cromwell and soon fell into disrepair. It is now cared for by English Heritage.

South Cumbria

BARROW-IN-FURNESS, PIEL CASTLE 1893 32991
Piel is one of three islands off the coast at Barrow, and is crowned by the ruined remains of 14th-century Piel Castle, which boasts the largest medieval keep in the north-west of England. The ruined castle is seen here from the shore at South Point.

CARK, THE BRIDGE 1897 40515
A quiet corner of the tiny village of Cark, where the River Eea flows under a low bridge into the sands of Morecambe Bay. Note the upturned cart by the bridge. The village takes its name from the Old Welsh 'carreg', meaning rock or stone.

CARTMEL, THE CROSS AND MARKET PLACE 1894 34105
Cartmel has been described as a cathedral city in miniature, and this corner of the cobbled Market Place has not changed much since this photograph was taken. The ancient Market Cross and village pump are watched over by the Cavendish Arms (left).

CARTMEL, CAVENDISH STREET 1914 67406
On the left, two locals discuss the forthcoming Exhibition Club of Cark-in-Cartmel, which would include sports in Holker Park, £25 in prizes and a dance. The cottage in the centre was Ayers Old-Fashioned Eating House, with plenty of seating outside for visitors.

South Cumbria

CARTMEL, DEVONSHIRE PLACE 1929 82776
The magnificent late 12th-century priory church of St Mary and St Michael dominates this view of Devonshire Place. Founded in 1190 by William Marshall, Baron of Cartmel and later 1st Earl of Pembroke, it was a priory of the Augustinian Order and still serves as the parish church.

CARTMEL, THE BECK 1914 67410
Ducks dabble peacefully in the beck which runs through the centre of the village, while a mother proudly poses with her baby. In the background, a notice on the shop advertises a 20 hp Ford car for hire.

FLOOKBURGH, THE VILLAGE 1897 40521
Flookburgh, a charming and ancient market town between the Kent Estuary and Cartmel Sands, takes its name from Floki, the name of a Norse settler. It was renowned for its cockle gatherers and fishing for flukes, or flat fish, in the estuary. In this view it is obvious that a photographer was a rare sight.

South Cumbria

FLOOKBURGH, THE KING'S ARMS 1903 50097
Post horses were still available for hire from George Fell at the King's Arms when this photograph was taken. But no one would dare leave a hand cart in the middle of the street today, as these children have!

GRANGE-OVER-SANDS, MAIN STREET 1894 34118
A horse and cart in the distance is wending its way up the hill. On the left of the picture is the Working Mens' Institute. Note the awnings over the shops (centre) to protect goods in the window from the sun.

GRANGE-OVER-SANDS, MAIN STREET c1955 G42087
This photograph was taken from almost exactly the same spot as photograph No 34118 about 60 years later, and the motor car has arrived! There are fewer awnings to be seen, but many other buildings are unchanged.

GRANGE-OVER-SANDS, THE BEACH 1912 64347
This fisherman is in reflective mood as he sits on his boat, the 'Dewdrop', and looks out over the fast-expanding township of Grange-over-Sands. Many wealthy business families from industrial Lancashire settled here as it became a fashionable seaside resort in the middle years of the 19th century.

South Cumbria

GRANGE-OVER-SANDS, THE PIER 1914 67426
Canvas-sailed boats are tied up at the pier; this was the time when Grange was becoming a popular seaside resort, famed as an escape from industrial Lancashire and for its bracing air and equable climate.

Francis Frith's Cumbria

South Cumbria

GRANGE-OVER-SANDS, THE RAILWAY 1929 82781
The coming of the railway to Grange-over-Sands in 1857 signalled the town's rapid expansion as a seaside resort for visitors from the industrial mill towns of Lancashire. Here engine No 12501 steams along the front, past the town's park, where the conical-roofed bandstand is prominent.

GREENODD, MAIN STREET 1921 70700
A local farmworker, dog at his feet and scythe over his shoulder, stands outside the Ship Inn as an early motor car (which looks suspiciously as if it has been superimposed) drives up the Main Street. The Ship Inn gives a clue to Greenodd's former importance as a port at the mouth of the River Leven.

GREENODD, THE VIADUCT 1921 70698
This railway viaduct crossed the peaceful estuary of the River Leven. It was demolished in the 1970s to make way for the A590, which bypassed the village of Greenodd.

South Cumbria

HAVERIGG, MAIN STREET c1950 H466012
A delivery van is parked outside the grocer's shop in the Main Street of the small cul-de-sac village of Haverigg. Haverigg is perhaps best known today for the nearby Hodbarrow Point RSPB reserve, which has been developed on a former iron mining site on the Duddon Estuary.

HAVERIGG, LAZY RIVER AND THE BRIDGE c1955 H466027
Four local men and their dogs discuss the forthcoming day's fishing by the Lazy River. 'Lazy River' must have been the local name for the local beck which runs into the Duddon Estuary by the white-painted Harbour Hotel, seen here across the river.

HOLKER, THE VILLAGE 1912 64388
Standing by the gatehouse to the 'Big House' - Holker Hall - these four local schoolchildren from Holker pose for the camera on a wet day. Holker is very much an estate village for workers on the estate of the Cavendish family who have been here since 1756. The Hall was originally built in the early 17th century.

HOLKER, THE HOLKER HALL ESTATE 1906 54587
Although originally captioned 'Holker Hall', this photograph actually shows one of the houses on the Holker Hall estate, which has been in the hands of the Cavendish family for over 200 years and is now the home of the Lakeland Motor Museum. The Hall is in a beautiful position, overlooking the Cartmel Sands and backed by the Furness Fells.

South Cumbria

KENTS BANK, FROM THE SANDS 1894 34127
New villas sprang up along the front at Kents Bank on the Kent Estuary as the village became popular as a holiday resort. Today, Kents Bank is perhaps best known as the starting or finishing point for guided crossings led by the Queen's Guide, Cedric Robinson, over the treacherous sands of Morecambe Bay.

KIRKBY-IN-FURNESS, BECKSIDE c1955 K114004
The tower of the parish church dominates this view of Beckside, a small hamlet on the slopes of the Furness Fells above the village of Kirkby-in-Furness on the Duddon Estuary. The estuary and the town of Millom on the far side can be seen in the distance.

MILLOM, WELLINGTON STREET c1955 M277046
The busy industrial village of Millom on the Duddon Estuary was founded on the wealth won from the iron ore discovered at nearby Hodbarrow in 1868. With the slopes of Black Combe and the Lakeland mountains to the north, Millom occupies an enviable position, and was the home of the Lakeland poet Norman Nicholson.

MILNTHORPE, THE SQUARE c1950 M263018
Sometimes known as Police Square, The Square at Milnthorpe is the natural centre and market place for this thriving village which grew up as a seaport on the River Bela, until the river silted up. The tower of the parish church of St Thomas, built in 1837 when Milnthorpe finally broke free of ecclesiastical ties with nearby Heversham, dominates.

South Cumbria

MILNTHORPE, THE CROSS ROADS c1955 M263020
The crossroads at Milnthorpe was well known to motorists travelling to Scotland or the Lake District on the A6 before the advent of the M6 motorway. Milnthorpe had been an important stopping place for north or southbound traffic since the 18th century, and there were numerous coaching inns along the main road.

SILECROFT, THE VILLAGE c1955 S657016
An empty village street in Silecroft, a small settlement at the foot of Black Combe, at 1,970ft the southernmost of the major Lake District hills and a fine viewpoint across the Irish Sea. Silecroft takes its name from the Old Norse and means 'the croft where the sallows grew'.

ESTABLISHED
1825
C.E.COURT.
LATE HIRD
JEWELLER
AND
OPTICIAN.
A.BARNES, GUNSMITH &
FISHING TACKLE MAKER
SPORTSMAN'S OUTFITTER.
C. E. Court. Silversmith.

South Cumbria

ULVERSTON, MARKET PLACE 1912 64395
At the time this photograph was taken, Ulverston was still a busy commercial port linked to the River Leven by the mile-long Ulverston Canal, England's shortest. It exported copper, iron, slate, barley, bobbins, gunpowder and leather all over the Empire.

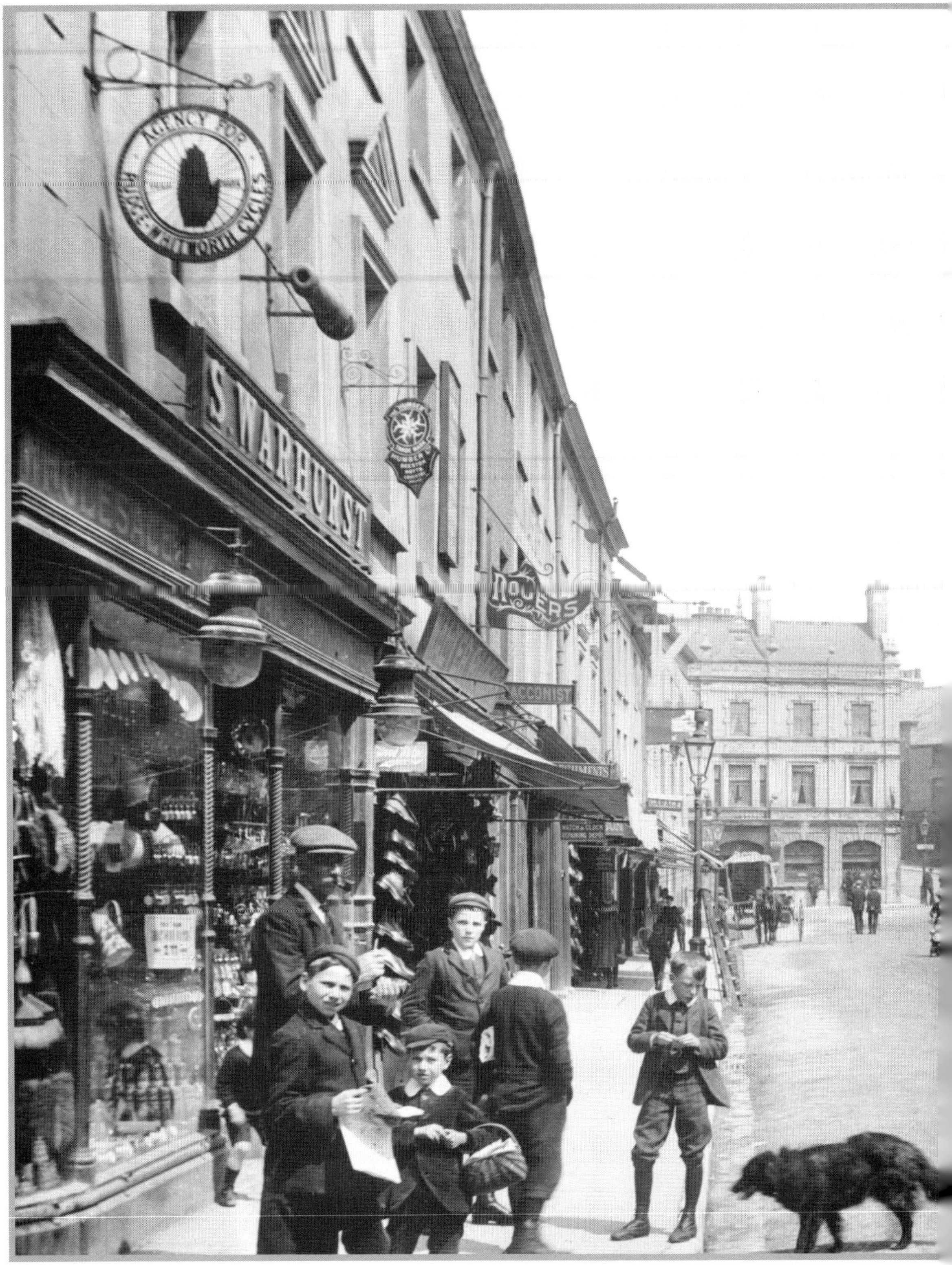
AGENCY FOR
S. WARHURST

ULVERSTON, KING STREET 1912 64396
Cloth-capped and gaitered Edwardian children stand with their father outside S Warhurst's hardware shop on a sunny day. Warhurst was an agent for Rudge Whitworth cycles, a popular form of leisure transport at the time. Across the road is John Smith's Umbrella Hospital.

ULVERSTON, MARKET PLACE 1912 64393
Ulverston was granted a market charter as early as 1280 by Edward I. The international aspect of the town's trade can be seen by the sign outside Joseph Hird's grocery in the centre of the picture. It advertises him as a 'French and Italian Warehouseman'.

ULVERSTON, NEW MARKET STREET 1912 64397
The name Birkett is prominent on several of the shops in this view. This prominent local family also produced the lawyer William Norman Birkett, created 1st Baron Birkett in 1958. Birkett was a Liberal MP in the 1920s who later represented Britain at the Nuremburg War Trials.

South Cumbria

ULVERSTON, HOAD HILL AND MONUMENT 1912 64403
The Hoad Hill Monument at Ulverston is a replica of the Eddystone Lighthouse, and was built as a memorial to Sir John Barrow, founder of the Royal Geographical Society and for 40 years Secretary to the Admiralty. Barrow was born in Ulverston in 1764.

Chapter Five: West Cumbria

BROUGHTON MOOR, MAIN STREET c1965 B830002
Broughton Moor is a former coal-mining township on the outskirts of Maryport in western Cumbria. In this photograph, local children play outside the Maryport Co-operative Industrial Society store in Broughton's Main Street, with the white-washed Central Stores prominent further down the street.

CLEATOR MOOR, THE SQUARE c1960 C568001
A group of residents wait patiently for the bus on the wide, rectangular Square. The Square is the natural focus of this former iron-mining town on the western fringe of Ennerdale and the Lake District hills.

West Cumbria

COCKERMOUTH, THE CHURCH 1906 55003
Cockermouth is best known as the birthplace of the poet William Wordsworth, and there is a stained glass window memorial to this fact in the parish church of All Saints. Wordsworth's father, an agent for the Lowther Estate at nearby Lowther Castle, is buried in the churchyard.

EGREMONT, THE TOWN HALL AND MAIN STREET c1960 E192010
The wide Main Street of Egremont, watched over by the clock tower of the Victorian Town Hall, is typical of many Cumbrian towns. Egremont was granted a market charter as early as 1267, and is famous for its Crab Apple Fair held every September, which includes the World Gurning (face-pulling) Championships.

ESKDALE GREEN c1955 E194033
The beautiful valley of Eskdale runs down from some of the highest ground in the Lake District to reach the sea at Ravenglass. Eskdale Green, a stop on the popular Ravenglass and Eskdale narrow gauge railway, is perhaps best known for its Outward Bound Mountain School, housed in this former Victorian mansion.

FRIZINGTON, MAIN STREET c1950 F183010
The village nonconformist chapel is prominent on the right of this photograph of Frizington, a large former coal mining village just inland from Whitehaven. Public street lighting was still by oil here until the early part of the 20th century.

West Cumbria

GOSFORTH, THE VILLAGE c1955 G262002
A couple of old villagers pass the time of day with a youngster in the West Cumbrian village of Gosforth. Gosforth is best known for its outstanding collection of Anglo-Saxon and Danish sculpture at the parish church of St Mary, the most famous of which is the intricately-carved 14ft high Gosforth Cross.

WORKINGTON, POW STREET c1960 W316031
Shoppers go about their business in this busy scene. Workington, on the mouth of the River Derwent, owes its growth mainly to the coal and steel industries, but it has always been slightly overshadowed by the larger town of Whitehaven to the south.

Francis Frith's Cumbria

WORKINGTON, MURRAY ROAD c1955 W316015
The grand facade of Cumberland Motor Services Bus Station dominates this photograph. At this time, of course, Workington was a county borough and one of the major service centres in the old county of Cumberland, which disappeared in 1974.

WORKINGTON, THE DOCKS c1950 W316027
Shipyards were recorded at Workington before 1756, and by 1829 it had two, along with Harrington and Maryport. The port also exported coal and iron from the local mines and iron smelting works which made this part of West Cumbria one of the major industrial centres of northern England.

Index

Abbeytown 48
Alston 66
Allithwaite 79
Ambleside 16-17, 18, 19, 20
Arnside 79, 80
Armathwaite 48
Aspatria 49
Bampton Grange 49
Barbon 67
Bardsea 81, 82
Barrow-in-Furness 83, 84-85, 86-87, 88, 89
Borrowdale 23, 24
Bowness 21, 22, 23
Brampton 50-51, 52
Brough 67
Brougham Castle 52
Broughton Moor 110
Burgh-by-Sands 53
Buttermere 24
Cark 89
Carlisle 54-55
Cartmel 90, 91
Cleator Moor 110
Cockermouth 111
Coldbeck 68
Coniston 25, 26-27, 28
Crummock Water 25
Dent 69
Derwent Water 28, 29
Egremont 111
Eskdale Green 112
Flookburgh 92, 93
Frizington 112
Furness Abbey 88
Garrigill 70

Gosforth 113
Grange-over-Sands 93, 94, 95, 96-97
Grasmere 30, 31
Greenodd 98
Greystoke 56, 57, 61
Haverigg 99
Hawkshead 32-33, 34, 35
Helvellyn 31
Holker 100
Kendal 35 36-37, 38, 39, 40
Kents Bank 101
Keswick 41
Kirkby in Furness 101
Kirkby Lonsdale 70, 71, 72-73, 74, 75
Kirkby Stephen 75
Lanercost Priory 57
Langdale Pikes 42-43, 44
Lazonby 76
Longtown 60
Maryport 58-59, 60
Millom 102
Milnthorpe 102, 103
Morland 76
Newby Bridge 44, 45
Penrith 62, 63
Sedbergh 77, 78
Silecroft 103
Silloth 64
Troutbeck 45
Ulverston 104-105, 106-107, 108, 109
Wetheral 64
Wigton 65
Windermere 46-47
Workington 113, 114

Frith Book Co Titles

www.francisfrith.co.uk

The Frith Book Company publishes over 100 new titles each year. A selection of those currently available are listed below. For latest catalogue please contact Frith Book Co.

Town Books 96 pages, approx 100 photos. County and Themed Books 128 pages, approx 150 photos (unless specified). All titles hardback laminated case and jacket except those indicated pb (paperback)

Title	ISBN	Price
Amersham, Chesham & Rickmansworth (pb)	1-85937-340-2	£9.99
Ancient Monuments & Stone Circles	1-85937-143-4	£17.99
Aylesbury (pb)	1-85937-227-9	£9.99
Bakewell	1-85937-113-2	£12.99
Barnstaple (pb)	1-85937-300-3	£9.99
Bath (pb)	1-85937419-0	£9.99
Bedford (pb)	1-85937-205-8	£9.99
Berkshire (pb)	1-85937-191-4	£9.99
Berkshire Churches	1-85937-170-1	£17.99
Blackpool (pb)	1-85937-382-8	£9.99
Bognor Regis (pb)	1-85937-431-x	£9.99
Bournemouth	1-85937-067-5	£12.99
Bradford (pb)	1-85937-204-x	£9.99
Brighton & Hove(pb)	1-85937-192-2	£8.99
Bristol (pb)	1-85937-264-3	£9.99
British Life A Century Ago (pb)	1-85937-213-9	£9.99
Buckinghamshire (pb)	1-85937-200-7	£9.99
Camberley (pb)	1-85937-222-8	£9.99
Cambridge (pb)	1-85937-422-0	£9.99
Cambridgeshire (pb)	1-85937-420-4	£9.99
Canals & Waterways (pb)	1-85937-291-0	£9.99
Canterbury Cathedral (pb)	1-85937-179-5	£9.99
Cardiff (pb)	1-85937-093-4	£9.99
Carmarthenshire	1-85937-216-3	£14.99
Chelmsford (pb)	1-85937-310-0	£9.99
Cheltenham (pb)	1-85937-095-0	£9.99
Cheshire (pb)	1-85937-271-6	£9.99
Chester	1-85937-090-x	£12.99
Chesterfield	1-85937-378-x	£9.99
Chichester (pb)	1-85937-228-7	£9.99
Colchester (pb)	1-85937-188-4	£8.99
Cornish Coast	1-85937-163-9	£14.99
Cornwall (pb)	1-85937-229-5	£9.99
Cornwall Living Memories	1-85937-248-1	£14.99
Cotswolds (pb)	1-85937-230-9	£9.99
Cotswolds Living Memories	1-85937-255-4	£14.99
County Durham	1-85937-123-x	£14.99
Croydon Living Memories	1-85937-162-0	£9.99
Cumbria	1-85937-101-9	£14.99
Dartmoor	1-85937-145-0	£14.99
Derby (pb)	1-85937-367-4	£9.99
Derbyshire (pb)	1-85937-196-5	£9.99
Devon (pb)	1-85937-297-x	£9.99
Dorset (pb)	1-85937-269-4	£9.99
Dorset Churches	1-85937-172-8	£17.99
Dorset Coast (pb)	1-85937-299-6	£9.99
Dorset Living Memories	1-85937-210-4	£14.99
Down the Severn	1-85937-118-3	£14.99
Down the Thames (pb)	1-85937-278-3	£9.99
Down the Trent	1-85937-311-9	£14.99
Dublin (pb)	1-85937-231-7	£9.99
East Anglia (pb)	1-85937-265-1	£9.99
East London	1-85937-080-2	£14.99
East Sussex	1-85937-130-2	£14.99
Eastbourne	1-85937-061-6	£12.99
Edinburgh (pb)	1-85937-193-0	£8.99
England in the 1880s	1-85937-331-3	£17.99
English Castles (pb)	1-85937-434-4	£9.99
English Country Houses	1-85937-161-2	£17.99
Essex (pb)	1-85937-270-8	£9.99
Exeter	1-85937-126-4	£12.99
Exmoor	1-85937-132-9	£14.99
Falmouth	1-85937-066-7	£12.99
Folkestone (pb)	1-85937-124-8	£9.99
Glasgow (pb)	1-85937-190-6	£9.99
Gloucestershire	1-85937-102-7	£14.99
Great Yarmouth (pb)	1-85937-426-3	£9.99
Greater Manchester (pb)	1-85937-266-x	£9.99
Guildford (pb)	1-85937-410-7	£9.99
Hampshire (pb)	1-85937-279-1	£9.99
Hampshire Churches (pb)	1-85937-207-4	£9.99
Harrogate	1-85937-423-9	£9.99
Hastings & Bexhill (pb)	1-85937-131-0	£9.99
Heart of Lancashire (pb)	1-85937-197-3	£9.99
Helston (pb)	1-85937-214-7	£9.99
Hereford (pb)	1-85937-175-2	£9.99
Herefordshire	1-85937-174-4	£14.99
Hertfordshire (pb)	1-85937-247-3	£9.99
Horsham (pb)	1-85937-432-8	£9.99
Humberside	1-85937-215-5	£14.99
Hythe, Romney Marsh & Ashford	1-85937-256-2	£9.99

Available from your local bookshop or from the publisher

Frith Book Co Titles (continued)

Title	ISBN	Price	Title	ISBN	Price
Ipswich (pb)	1-85937-424-7	£9.99	St Ives (pb)	1-85937415-8	£9.99
Ireland (pb)	1-85937-181-7	£9.99	Scotland (pb)	1-85937-182-5	£9.99
Isle of Man (pb)	1-85937-268-6	£9.99	Scottish Castles (pb)	1-85937-323-2	£9.99
Isles of Scilly	1-85937-136-1	£14.99	Sevenoaks & Tunbridge	1-85937-057-8	£12.99
Isle of Wight (pb)	1-85937-429-8	£9.99	Sheffield, South Yorks (pb)	1-85937-267-8	£9.99
Isle of Wight Living Memories	1-85937-304-6	£14.99	Shrewsbury (pb)	1-85937-325-9	£9.99
Kent (pb)	1-85937-189-2	£9.99	Shropshire (pb)	1-85937-326-7	£9.99
Kent Living Memories	1-85937-125-6	£14.99	Somerset	1-85937-153-1	£14.99
Lake District (pb)	1-85937-275-9	£9.99	South Devon Coast	1-85937-107-8	£14.99
Lancaster, Morecambe & Heysham (pb)	1-85937-233-3	£9.99	South Devon Living Memories	1-85937-168-x	£14.99
Leeds (pb)	1-85937-202-3	£9.99	South Hams	1-85937-220-1	£14.99
Leicester	1-85937-073-x	£12.99	Southampton (pb)	1-85937-427-1	£9.99
Leicestershire (pb)	1-85937-185-x	£9.99	Southport (pb)	1-85937-425-5	£9.99
Lincolnshire (pb)	1-85937-433-6	£9.99	Staffordshire	1-85937-047-0	£12.99
Liverpool & Merseyside (pb)	1-85937-234-1	£9.99	Stratford upon Avon	1-85937-098-5	£12.99
London (pb)	1-85937-183-3	£9.99	Suffolk (pb)	1-85937-221-x	£9.99
Ludlow (pb)	1-85937-176-0	£9.99	Suffolk Coast	1-85937-259-7	£14.99
Luton (pb)	1-85937-235-x	£9.99	Surrey (pb)	1-85937-240-6	£9.99
Maidstone	1-85937-056-x	£14.99	Sussex (pb)	1-85937-184-1	£9.99
Manchester (pb)	1-85937-198-1	£9.99	Swansea (pb)	1-85937-167-1	£9.99
Middlesex	1-85937-158-2	£14.99	Tees Valley & Cleveland	1-85937-211-2	£14.99
New Forest	1-85937-128-0	£14.99	Thanet (pb)	1-85937-116-7	£9.99
Newark (pb)	1-85937-366-6	£9.99	Tiverton (pb)	1-85937-178-7	£9.99
Newport, Wales (pb)	1-85937-258-9	£9.99	Torbay	1-85937-063-2	£12.99
Newquay (pb)	1-85937-421-2	£9.99	Truro	1-85937-147-7	£12.99
Norfolk (pb)	1-85937-195-7	£9.99	Victorian and Edwardian Cornwall	1-85937-252-x	£14.99
Norfolk Living Memories	1-85937-217-1	£14.99	Victorian & Edwardian Devon	1-85937-253-8	£14.99
Northamptonshire	1-85937-150-7	£14.99	Victorian & Edwardian Kent	1-85937-149-3	£14.99
Northumberland Tyne & Wear (pb)	1-85937-281-3	£9.99	Vic & Ed Maritime Album	1-85937-144-2	£17.99
North Devon Coast	1-85937-146-9	£14.99	Victorian and Edwardian Sussex	1-85937-157-4	£14.99
North Devon Living Memories	1-85937-261-9	£14.99	Victorian & Edwardian Yorkshire	1-85937-154-x	£14.99
North London	1-85937-206-6	£14.99	Victorian Seaside	1-85937-159-0	£17.99
North Wales (pb)	1-85937-298-8	£9.99	Villages of Devon (pb)	1-85937-293-7	£9.99
North Yorkshire (pb)	1-85937-236-8	£9.99	Villages of Kent (pb)	1-85937-294-5	£9.99
Norwich (pb)	1-85937-194-9	£8.99	Villages of Sussex (pb)	1-85937-295-3	£9.99
Nottingham (pb)	1-85937-324-0	£9.99	Warwickshire (pb)	1-85937-203-1	£9.99
Nottinghamshire (pb)	1-85937-187-6	£9.99	Welsh Castles (pb)	1-85937-322-4	£9.99
Oxford (pb)	1-85937-411-5	£9.99	West Midlands (pb)	1-85937-289-9	£9.99
Oxfordshire (pb)	1-85937-430-1	£9.99	West Sussex	1-85937-148-5	£14.99
Peak District (pb)	1-85937-280-5	£9.99	West Yorkshire (pb)	1-85937-201-5	£9.99
Penzance	1-85937-069-1	£12.99	Weymouth (pb)	1-85937-209-0	£9.99
Peterborough (pb)	1-85937-219-8	£9.99	Wiltshire (pb)	1-85937-277-5	£9.99
Piers	1-85937-237-6	£17.99	Wiltshire Churches (pb)	1-85937-171-x	£9.99
Plymouth	1-85937-119-1	£12.99	Wiltshire Living Memories	1-85937-245-7	£14.99
Poole & Sandbanks (pb)	1-85937-251-1	£9.99	Winchester (pb)	1-85937-428-x	£9.99
Preston (pb)	1-85937-212-0	£9.99	Windmills & Watermills	1-85937-242-2	£17.99
Reading (pb)	1-85937-238-4	£9.99	Worcester (pb)	1-85937-165-5	£9.99
Romford (pb)	1-85937-319-4	£9.99	Worcestershire	1-85937-152-3	£14.99
Salisbury (pb)	1-85937-239-2	£9.99	York (pb)	1-85937-199-x	£9.99
Scarborough (pb)	1-85937-379-8	£9.99	Yorkshire (pb)	1-85937-186-8	£9.99
St Albans (pb)	1-85937-341-0	£9.99	Yorkshire Living Memories	1-85937-166-3	£14.99

See Frith books on the internet www.francisfrith.co.uk

Frith Products & Services

Francis Frith would doubtless be pleased to know that the pioneering publishing venture he started in 1860 still continues today. A hundred and forty years later, The Francis Frith Collection continues in the same innovative tradition and is now one of the foremost publishers of vintage photographs in the world. Some of the current activities include:

Interior Decoration

Today Frith's photographs can be seen framed and as giant wall murals in thousands of pubs, restaurants, hotels, banks, retail stores and other public buildings throughout the country. In every case they enhance the unique local atmosphere of the places they depict and provide reminders of gentler days in an increasingly busy and frenetic world.

Product Promotions

Frith products are used by many major companies to promote the sales of their own products or to reinforce their own history and heritage. Frith promotions have been used by Hovis bread, Courage beers, Scots Porage Oats, Colman's mustard, Cadbury's foods, Mellow Birds coffee, Dunhill pipe tobacco, Guinness, and Bulmer's Cider.

Genealogy and Family History

As the interest in family history and roots grows world-wide, more and more people are turning to Frith's photographs of Great Britain for images of the towns, villages and streets where their ancestors lived; and, of course, photographs of the churches and chapels where their ancestors were christened, married and buried are an essential part of every genealogy tree and family album.

Frith Products

All Frith photographs are available Framed or just as Mounted Prints and Posters (size 23 x 16 inches). These may be ordered from the address below. From time to time other products - Address Books, Calendars, Table Mats, etc - are available.

The Internet

Already twenty thousand Frith photographs can be viewed and purchased on the internet through the Frith websites and a myriad of partner sites.

For more detailed information on Frith companies and products, look at these sites:

www.francisfrith.co.uk
www.francisfrith.com
(for North American visitors)

See the complete list of Frith Books at:
www.francisfrith.co.uk

This web site is regularly updated with the latest list of publications from the Frith Book Company. If you wish to buy books relating to another part of the country that your local bookshop does not stock, you may purchase on-line.

For further information, trade, or author enquiries please contact us at the address below:
The Francis Frith Collection, Frith's Barn, Teffont, Salisbury, Wiltshire, England SP3 5QP.
Tel: +44 (0)1722 716 376 Fax: +44 (0)1722 716 881 Email: sales@francisfrith.co.uk

See Frith books on the internet www.francisfrith.co.uk

TO RECEIVE YOUR FREE MOUNTED PRINT

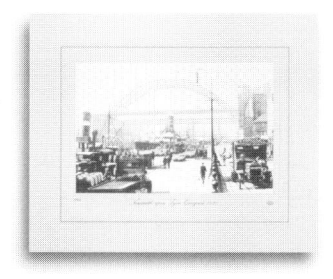

Mounted Print
Overall size 14 x 11 inches

Cut out this Voucher and return it with your remittance for £1.95 to cover postage and handling, to UK addresses. For overseas addresses please include £4.00 post and handling. Choose any photograph included in this book. Your SEPIA print will be A4 in size, and mounted in a cream mount with burgundy rule line, overall size 14 x 11 inches.

Order additional Mounted Prints at HALF PRICE (only £7.49 each*)

If there are further pictures you would like to order, possibly as gifts for friends and family, purchase them at half price (no additional postage and handling required).

Have your Mounted Prints framed*

For an additional £14.95 per print you can have your chosen Mounted Print framed in an elegant polished wood and gilt moulding, overall size 16 x 13 inches (no additional postage and handling required).

---
* IMPORTANT!
These special prices are only available if ordered using the original voucher on this page (no copies permitted) and at the same time as your free Mounted Print, for delivery to the same address

---

Frith Collectors' Guild

From time to time we publish a magazine of news and stories about Frith photographs and further special offers of Frith products. If you would like 12 months FREE membership, please return this form.

Send completed forms to:
**The Francis Frith Collection,
Frith's Barn, Teffont, Salisbury,
Wiltshire SP3 5QP**

Voucher for FREE and Reduced Price Frith Prints

Picture no.	Page number	Qty	Mounted @ £7.49	Framed + £14.95	Total Cost
		1	Free of charge*	£	£
			£7.49	£	£
			£7.49	£	£
			£7.49	£	£
			£7.49	£	£
			£7.49	£	£

Please allow 28 days for delivery   *** Post & handling**   **£1.95**

Book Title ....   **Total Order Cost**   **£**

Please do not photocopy this voucher. Only the original is valid, so please cut it out and return it to us.

I enclose a cheque / postal order for £ ....
made payable to 'The Francis Frith Collection'
OR please debit my Mastercard / Visa / Switch / Amex card
(credit cards please on all overseas orders)

Number ....

Issue No (Switch only) .... Valid from (Amex/Switch) ....

Expires .... Signature ....

Name Mr/Mrs/Ms ....

Address ....

....

.... Postcode ....

Daytime Tel No ....   Valid to 31/12/03

The Francis Frith Collectors' Guild

Please enrol me as a member for 12 months free of charge.

Name Mr/Mrs/Ms ....

Address ....

....

....

.... Postcode ....

Free Print - see overleaf

Would you like to find out more about Francis Frith?

We have recently recruited some entertaining speakers who are happy to visit local groups, clubs and societies to give an illustrated talk documenting Frith's travels and photographs. If you are a member of such a group and are interested in hosting a presentation, we would love to hear from you.

Our speakers bring with them a small selection of our local town and county books, together with sample prints. They are happy to take orders. A small proportion of the order value is donated to the group who have hosted the presentation. The talks are therefore an excellent way of fundraising for small groups and societies.

Can you help us with information about any of the Frith photographs in this book?

We are gradually compiling an historical record for each of the photographs in the Frith archive. It is always fascinating to find out the names of the people shown in the pictures, as well as insights into the shops, buildings and other features depicted.

If you recognize anyone in the photographs in this book, or if you have information not already included in the author's caption, do let us know. We would love to hear from you, and will try to publish it in future books or articles.

Our production team

Frith books are produced by a small dedicated team at offices in the converted Grade II listed 18th-century barn at Teffont near Salisbury, illustrated above. Most have worked with the Frith Collection for many years. All have in common one quality: they have a passion for the Frith Collection. The team is constantly expanding, but currently includes:

Jason Buck, John Buck, Douglas Burns, Heather Crisp, Lucy Elcock, Isobel Hall, Rob Hames, Hazel Heaton, Peter Horne, James Kinnear, Tina Leary, Hannah Marsh, Eliza Sackett, Terence Sackett, Sandra Sanger, Lewis Taylor, Shelley Tolcher, Helen Vimpany, Clive Wathen and Jenny Wathen.